Did You

ESSEX

A MISCELLANY

Compiled by Julia Skinner

With particular reference to the work of Frances Clamp
and Russell Thompson

THE FRANCIS FRITH COLLECTION

www.francisfrith.com

First published in the United Kingdom in 2011 by The Francis Frith Collection®

This edition published exclusively for Bradwell Books in 2013
For trade enquiries see: www.bradwellbooks.com or tel: 0800 834 920
ISBN 978-1-84589-567-9

British Library Cataloguing in Publication Data

Did You Know? Essex - A Miscellany
Compiled by Julia Skinner
With particular reference to the work of Frances Clamp and Russell Thompson

The Francis Frith Collection
6 Oakley Business Park,
Wylye Road, Dinton,
Wiltshire SP3 5EU
Tel: +44 (0) 1722 716 376
Email: info@francisfrith.co.uk
www.francisfrith.com

Printed and bound in Malaysia
Contains material sourced from responsibly managed forests

Front Cover: **JAYWICK, A 'B' TYPE BUNGALOW c1955** J4027p
Frontispiece: **CHELSMFORD, HIGH STREET 1895** 35514

The colour-tinting is for illustrative purposes only, and is not intended to be historically accurate

CONTENTS

INTRODUCTION

Essex is steeped in history, with beautiful towns and villages, and some of the most notable churches to be found anywhere in England. The county covers 3,670 square kilometres (1,417 square miles). It is roughly square in shape, with its boundaries mainly defined by water: the River Stour to the north, the Rivers Stort and Lea (or Lee) to the west, the mighty Thames to the south, and the North Sea to the east. On the southern border, beside the River Thames, are the busy towns of Purfleet, Grays and the port of Tilbury. Eastwards along the Thames estuary lie the brooding ruins of Hadleigh Castle and the old fishing village of Leigh-on-Sea, and then the bustling brightness of Southend, with its famous pier stretching out into the estuary. Along the eastern, North Sea, coast of the county, the creeks and salt marshes of the region around the Rivers Crouch and Blackwater have their own wild beauty, where sinuous tideways finger far inland under the huge dome of the sky and break up the land, making the whole area difficult of access save by boat. Northwards is the major seaside town of Clacton, and yet further north lies the port of Harwich, now a gateway to the Continent. Moving inland to the centre of the county we come to the large, busy towns of historic Colchester, Braintree, Brentwood and Saffron Walden, and the administrative centre of the county, Chelmsford. Then, too, there are the modern 'new towns' of Basildon and Harlow.

Beyond its south-west fringe adjoining the London boroughs and the industrial Thames-side, much of Essex remains a land of small towns, of widely-spaced villages and tiny hamlets that have seen little change, one feels, since the Middle Ages. Many of the century-old scenes pictured in this book are immediately recognisable and little changed. Even today, the visitor has the sensation of revisiting an earlier age along many of the county's byways. The landscape is not generally flat; it includes the rolling hills along the Suffolk border, while in the south of the county such little eminences as Danbury and Laindon rise from the surrounding undulating land with such abruptness as to appear far more lofty than many a great hill elsewhere. This is English farmland at its best, a satisfying rural scene with clumps of trees, small woodlands and individual oaks and ashes breaking the view presided over by hurrying skies. It is still possible to be a few hundred yards from the edge of an Essex town, and yet ostensibly be in the middle of the countryside.

MALDON, A BARGE AT BEELEIGH 1906 55547x

ESSEX DIALECT
WORDS AND PHRASES

'Bald' - white-faced animals, as in pub names such as 'The Baldfaced Stag'.

'Barmed' - dirtied with mud.

'Clung' - lumps of wet mud or freshly dug earth.

'Dew' - if (but also used for 'if not').

'Dodman' - a name for a snail, and thus used for a lazy person or animal.

'Gant', or **'gantway'** - an alleyway between houses.

'Pollywags' - tadpoles.

'Rooning' - gathering mushrooms.

'Slud' - sludgy mud.

'Sobbled' - soaked, as in wet clothes.

'Venturemous' - bold, brave.

'Twitchell' - an alleyway.

'Tye' - a village green, as in the placename of Matching Tye.

'The hammer of it' - the long and the short of it.

HAUNTED ESSEX

The Red Lion Hotel in the centre of Colchester is reputed to have two ghosts, one is of a young girl which haunts the kitchen, and the other is believed to be of a monk who died in a fire. Another building in Colchester that may be haunted is Hollytrees Museum, where some staff have heard mysterious footsteps and the sound of someone playing a piano, as well as reporting the unexplained smell of perfume.

The Bear Inn at Stock, north of Billericay, is famous for the exploits of Charlie 'Spider' Marshall, a 19th-century ostler at the inn. For the price of a drink, he would shimmy up the chimney in one bar and come down in another. One day he failed to descend: his body was found 20 years later, in a small bacon-loft where the two chimneys meet. Not surprisingly, his ghost is said to roam the building and several landlords have reported seeing his shade.

The building on the southern corner of Waterloo Lane in Chelmsford – Bank Chambers – was built in the 1890s on the site of the White Horse Inn. It is allegedly haunted by the ghost of Thomas Kidderminster, an Ely farmer who was murdered by the innkeeper in 1654. His body was buried in the inn yard and was not discovered for several years.

In 1964, old Basildonians were wary of a mischievous ghost that haunted the southern end of Church Road near the present Swan Mead School. The ghost was said to pick people up and throw them over the hedge into fields near the Clay Hill Road. A coach and four with a headless driver is also supposed to speed down Church Road on occasions, and in 1964 there were reports of a ghostly crimson-gowned monk which had been seen shuffling across Church Road into Holy Cross churchyard.

The Cross Keys Hotel in Saffron Walden is reputed to be haunted by a ghostly Cavalier of the Civil War of the 17th century; his ghost is also said to roam along King Street.

ESSEX MISCELLANY

With the collapse of Roman rule over Britain in the early fifth century, the area now called Essex was in the forefront of the Anglo-Saxon colonisation of what became 'Angle-land' – England – and a Saxon kingdom was set up in the area. The county's name dates from this time, meaning 'the land of the East Saxons'. This Saxon heritage is recalled not only in the name of the county but also with the three peculiarly-shaped swords on the Essex County Council coat of arms: they are seaxes, the short, curved knives used by the Saxons. Appearing on everything from civic buildings to cricket clubs, they form a link to the county's distant past. The kings of the East Saxons were part-pagan, part-Christian characters whose names all began with the letter S – their dynasty claimed direct descent from their god Saxnot.

In 2003 one of the most exciting discoveries in British archaeology was made at Southend, when the undisturbed burial chamber of a Saxon king was discovered in land to the north-east of Priory Park in Prittlewell. The chambered tomb was dug into the ground and lined with wood, and filled with grave goods of such quality and value that the person buried there must have been a king of the East Saxons. Amongst the items found were a huge cauldron, flagons and bowls, probably symbolic of the grand feasts that the king had been wealthy enough to hold during his life, as well as personal possessions including a lyre, drinking vessels and a gaming set. Items found with the body appear to show that the king had been a Christian: his belt buckle was a reliquary (for holding holy relics), and two gold crosses had been placed beside his head. The grave dates from the early seventh century, and it is suggested that the king in the burial chamber was Saebert, the first East Saxon king to be converted to Christianity, who died cAD616.

The Saxons left quite a legacy in Essex. They left their names in the names of their villages, such as Stebbing ('the village of Stybba's people'), for example; they left churches and earthworks. Look at a map of Witham, for instance, and see how the ramparts of the Saxon hill-fort, or 'burh', at Chipping Hill are followed by the shapes of streets in the town. It was at Chipping Hill that the medieval settlement of Witham developed, the church of St Nicholas being located close to the earthwork.

In AD991 a force of East Saxons was defeated by Viking raiders in the disastrous Battle of Maldon, beside the River Blackwater. The Ealdorman Byrthnoth of Essex, with the local 'fyrd' (militia), went to do battle with the raiders but was killed. His thegns fought to the last man round their leader's body, and their heroism was commemorated in the greatest of all Anglo-Saxon battle-poems, 'The Battle of Maldon', that was composed not long after the event.

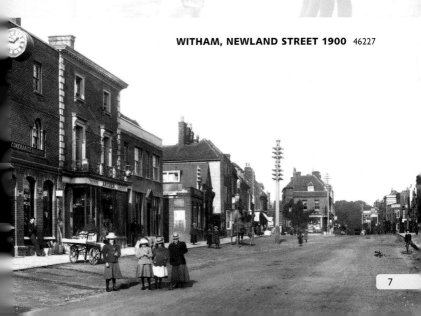

WITHAM, NEWLAND STREET 1900 46227

COLCHESTER, THE CASTLE 1908 60773

After the Norman Conquest of 1066, a number of important castles were built in the county. Many of them are now ruined, such as Hadleigh, but Essex's two great fortresses at Colchester and Castle Hedingham still remain. The magnificent Colchester Castle was constructed in 1080; it is the biggest Norman keep ever built, either here or in France, and was once four storeys high. Although the number of storeys was reduced in the 1680s, it is still an imposing and impressive building, with a floor plan half as big again as the White Tower of the Tower of London. The castle was used as a prison in the 18th century, and then a museum. In 1892 the castle grounds were opened as a public park, and in 1920 Viscount Cowdray bought the park and the castle and gave it to the town. The castle now houses a museum of Roman artefacts.

The four-storeyed Norman keep of the castle at Castle Hedingham (north of Braintree) is all that remains of what was one of Essex's greatest medieval fortresses, but is still impressive; it was built in the 1140s by Aubrey de Vere, whose father had fought at the battle of Hastings in 1066. The castle remained a stronghold of the de Veres, later the Earls of Oxford, for 550 years, and is still owned by a descendant. A feature of the castle is the magnificent banqueting hall and minstrels' gallery.

CASTLE HEDINGHAM, THE KEEP c1960 C238005

The Middle Ages and the Tudor era saw parts of Essex, notably the northern half, wax prosperous in agriculture, wool, textiles and many other industries, including cutlery.

There was a thriving cutlery industry in medieval Thaxted and the cutlers became the dominant force in the parish. At the end of the 14th century they built a magnificent Guildhall from which they could govern the town. One of the grandest churches in Essex must be the church of St John the Baptist, St Mary and St Lawrence in Thaxted, built from the profits of the cutlery trade – St Lawrence is the patron saint of cutlers. The spire can be seen soaring above the houses behind the Guildhall in the photograph below.

The building now called The Manse in Town Street in Thaxted was the home of the composer Gustav Holst between 1917 and 1925. So deep was Holst's affection for the town that he named a tune after the place: he adapted a setting for part of 'Jupiter' in his suite 'The Planets' to make a tune he called 'Thaxted'; it is familiar to many people as the tune for the hymn 'I Vow To Thee My Country'.

THAXTED, THE OLD GUILDHALL c1955 T28045

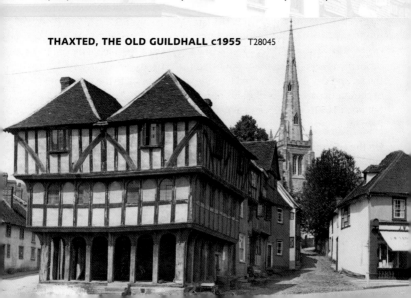

SAFFRON WALDEN, HIGH STREET 1919 69134

Saffron Walden got its name from the saffron obtained from the stamens of the crocus 'sativus' which was cultivated in great numbers by 'crockers' around the town in the later Middle Ages. Saffron produced an expensive yellow dye that was used for dying woollen cloth; it was also used in cookery and was thought to have medicinal properties. So important was saffron to the town that depictions of the saffron crocus were carved into the arcade opposite the door of the south porch of its glorious parish church of St Mary, built between 1450 and 1525, and a magnificent example of the later Perpendicular/early Tudor style.

On the Common at Saffron Walden is a medieval turf maze, a labyrinth of connecting pathways. Only eight such mazes survive in England, and this is the largest.

Chaters Hill in Saffron Walden is named after William Chater, a horticulturist who set up a plant nursery there in the 1820s where he perfected a strain of double and semi-double hollyhocks. They are commemorated in the name of Hollyhock Road in the town.

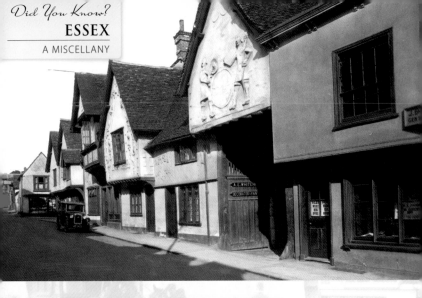

SAFFRON WALDEN, OLD SUN INN, CHURCH STREET 1932 85121

The Old Sun Inn in Saffron Walden (see above) features some of the best pargetting (decorative plasterwork) in East Anglia. The two figures in the pargework over the archway represent Tom Hickathrift and the Wisbech Giant, characters from East Anglian folklore, squaring up for their legendary fight. Tom Hickathrift is armed only with the axle of his cart and carries a little shield, while the Giant wields a great club. (Tom won.) The pargetting was done in 1676, which is why the figures are in 17th-century costume.

The magnificent mansion of Audley End on the outskirts of Saffron Walden was built in 1603-16 for Thomas Howard, 1st Earl of Suffolk and Lord Treasurer of England. When it was first built, Audley End was twice the size it is now; on seeing it, King James I is reputed to have dryly remarked that it was 'Too large for a king, but might do well for a Lord Treasurer'. In 1614 Thomas Howard was tried for embezzling public funds and fined £30,000; some of his ill-gotten gains had gone towards the building of Audley End.

At the corner of Chelmsford Road and Braintree Road in Felsted is Boote House, now a restaurant. An intriguing feature of the house is the carved figure of a grotesque woman with cloven hooves on the corner of the house; she appears to be wearing a chastity belt, or some sort of restraining iron girdle. George Boote designed and built the house himself in 1596. He probably put the figure there to ward off evil, but it has been unkindly suggested that she is a representation of his wife! She is known as 'The Hag of Felsted' or 'The Felsted Witch'. According to local folklore, she comes to life at Halloween and wanders the streets of the village.

The smallest windmill in Essex can be found in Haverhill Road at Finchingfield. Dating from at least the 1750s, it is a splendid example of an early post mill with a wooden windshaft, and is open to the public occasionally during the summer.

One of the more unusual attractions at Stansted Mountfitchet (between Saffron Walden and Harlow) is the House on the Hill Toy Museum, claimed to be the largest toy museum in Europe. The museum holds over 80,000 toys, some dating back to the Victorian era but mostly from the 1950s to the 1980s. Amongs the items you will find in the museum are a bicycle that belonged to Diana, Princess of Wales as a child.

The village of Matching Green, east of Harlow, is known for its ancient Marriage Feast Room, a large upper floor room of a jettied, timber-framed building next to the parish church; local lore says the building was erected by William Chimney in the 1480s to provide a place for the poor of the parish to hold their wedding feasts. There are only four such buildings surviving in England, and the Feast Room at Matching Green is the only example that has not been converted into a private residence. It is used for parochial and social functions within the village, but is not open to the public at other times.

The Dunmow Flitch takes place every four years in Great Dunmow, in which a flitch of bacon – a whole side of a pig – is presented to a married couple who have not, in the past 366 days, 'offended each other in deed or in word', nor in any way regretted their marriage. The event dates from very early times. The ceremony of the Dunmow Flitch Trials involves tongue-in-cheek court officials and a jury of 'six maidens and six bachelors'. A Judge assesses the claims of the vying couples, and claimants are quizzed on various aspects of their nuptial harmony. The winning couple are then carried through the town in the Flitch Chair. Central to the ceremony is the flitch of bacon itself. Here it is in this photograph, being paraded through the town, hung from a frame and draped with greenery.

GREAT DUNMOW, THE DUNMOW FLITCH 2000 D90706

What is believed to be the oldest surviving church in England is in Essex, the Chapel of St Peter-on-the-Walls at Bradwell-on-Sea, at the mouth of the Blackwater estuary. St Peter's was established by St Cedd, a Northumbrian missionary who came to the area in the mid seventh century to bring Christianity to the pagan Anglo-Saxons. It has survived various alternative uses, including roles as a lighthouse and a farm barn.

St Andrew's Church at Greensted near Ongar has walls made of vertical oak tree trunks, split and with the flat side facing inwards. Originally these were set into a massive beam, but in the mid 19th century this beam was replaced with brick supports. The timbers are original, and some have been dated to AD850, making this the oldest wooden church in England surviving from Saxon times.

An interesting feature of St Mary's Church in Great Baddow is a corbel on the wall of the west end which is a carved stone head of a woman wearing a scold's bridle, probably put there as a warning to women not to gossip or spread slander.

The village of Little Maplestead was granted to the Knights Hospitaller in the 12th century. The Knights Hospitaller was a military monastic order (called in full the Order of the Hospital of St John of Jerusalem) founded in the 11th century to give military protection and hospital care to pilgrims to the Holy Land during the crusades. In the 1340s the Knights Hospitaller built the church of St John the Baptist at Maplestead. They modelled it on the plan of the church of the Holy Sepulchre at Jerusalem, that is, it is circular, discounting the chancel and the porch. There are only four other churches of this sort in England. When the order of the Knights Hospitaller was dissolved in the 16th century, this building became the village's parish church.

Harlow as we know it today was the first London-area new town to result from the Town and Country Planning Act of 1946, a long-term plan to build a number of new towns around London to ease the housing crisis after the Second World War, when thousands of London families had lost their homes. The small village that was there before the new town arrived is known as Old Harlow, just to the east of the new town; its parish church has the largest collection of memorial brasses in the county. The 'new town' of Harlow was developed from 1949 onwards on the site of four sparsely-inhabited parishes, a little to the west of the 'old town' of Harlow. So many young families moved to Harlow New Town that in the 1960s it was given the nickname of 'Pram Town' because of the number of prams and pushchairs that could be seen there. The new town was admired for its sense of space and use of striking modern sculpture. The photo on the opposite page shows a cast bronze statue by Ralph Brown which has stood in the Market Square since 1960.

Britain's first modern-style residential tower block was built in the 'new town' of Harlow in 1951; known as The Lawns, it is now a Grade II listed building.

The first of Harlow New Town's pubs was opened at The Stow in the Mark Hall neighbourhood, in 1952. It is called the Essex Skipper, and it began the delightful tradition of naming all seventeen new pubs in Harlow after butterflies. Harlow's oldest pub is probably the Green Man at Mulberry Green in Old Harlow, once a coaching inn.

The name of Mulberry Green does not derive from a mulberry tree (although one was planted there in 1901 to mark the coronation of Edward VII, and another one was planted to mark the coronation of Queen Elizabeth II in 1953), but is believed to come from the Saxon words 'mot beorgh', meaning 'meeting place'.

HARLOW, 'THE MEAT PORTERS' STATUE c1965 H22103

WALTHAM ABBEY, MARKET SQUARE 1921 70158

An abbey was founded at what is now the town of Waltham Abbey in the 11th century. Later, King Edward the Confessor gave the manor of Waltham to the Anglo-Saxon Earl Harold Godwinson, who rebuilt the abbey church. Earl Harold subsequently became the King Harold who was killed at the battle of Hastings in 1066 in the Norman Conquest, and legend has it that his body was brought to Waltham for burial near to the High Altar of the abbey. Harold's church was refounded in the 12th century, and Waltham's abbey grew to be the richest monastery in Essex. Henry VIII had great affection for Waltham and it was the last monastic house to be closed down in his Dissolution; when the abbey was eventually dissolved in 1540, the people of the town saved its nave for use as their parish church. The reputed spot of King Harold's grave is marked by a stone slab in the churchyard, on the site of the high altar of the abbey church.

The notorious highwayman Dick Turpin was an Essex man, born in the village of Hempstead, east of Saffron Walden. He was born at the village inn, the Bluebell, where his father John Turpin was the landlord as well as a local butcher, and was baptised in the parish church on 21st September 1705. Before he turned to a career of highway robbery, Dick Turpin followed his father into the butcher's trade; he possibly worked as a butcher in Thaxted, and after marrying his wife Elizabeth c1725 he moved to Buckhurst Hill, where he opened a butcher's shop. It was almost certainly here that he first became involved with the 'Essex Gang', who were poaching deer in Waltham Forest – as a butcher, Turpin probably helped dispose of the carcasses. By the end of 1734 he had become an active member of the Essex Gang, which had now turned from poaching to armed robbery. Dick Turpin was eventually apprehended in east Yorkshire in 1738, using the alias of John Palmer. He was arrested for causing a fracas in the street and threatening behaviour and held at Beverley, but as he was also suspected of horse-theft he was transferred to York Castle to be tried at the Assizes. It was there that his true identity was discovered, and he was tried for his many crimes, including murder. He spent his final days in the condemned cell of York's prison before being hanged.

The great Forest of Essex once stretched from the Wash to the Thames. Over the years its size has diminished, but there are still large areas of woodland at Epping and Hatfield Broad Oak. Epping Forest was formerly known as Waltham Forest, and a third of the remaining forest land lies within the parish of Waltham Abbey. In 1878 the woods were handed over to the control of the Corporation of London, and in 1882 Queen Victoria announced that the forest should be dedicated for the use and enjoyment of her people for all time. An ancient right of the forest claimed by local people was that they could lop wood for winter fuel, provided the right was exercised by midnight on 11th November. In the 1860s a local landowner tried to trick the loppers with a supper at the Kings Head in Loughton on the same day, hoping that the men would lose track of time and lose the right; but he was out-foxed by one of the loppers, Thomas Willingale, who realised what was happening and managed to lop a single branch before the allotted hour, and kept the right going for a few more years. However, after taking control of the forest in 1878 the Corporation of London was determined to preserve and protect the forest from the depredations of the loppers, and in the 1880s it bought out the lopping rights from the local people; some of the compensation money was used to build Lopping Hall in the centre of Loughton, so-named in memory of that ancient right.

Bordered by Epping and Hainault Forests, Chigwell is often regarded as the first 'village' one encounters on leaving London. The King's Head at Chigwell was immortalised by Charles Dickens as The Maypole in his novel 'Barnaby Rudge', where it was described as having 'more gable ends than a lazy man would care to count on a sunny day'. Dickens borrowed the name from a Maypole Inn at nearby Chigwell Row. He later admitted that he had used writer's license, combining a description of the one house with the location of the other.

Brentwood was originally a settlement in the Forest of Essex that developed into a town because it was on the route that pilgrims took to cross the Thames on their way to the shrine of St Thomas the Martyr (Thomas Becket) at Canterbury. The link with St Thomas of Canterbury and Brentwood is retained with the dedication of the town's present parish church of St Thomas the Martyr which was built in the 1880s in Victorian Gothic style. The stone carvings around the west door of the church, to the south of the tower, depict the four evangelists standing on either side of the door. Beneath his feet each one has his symbol: an angel/man for St Matthew, a lion for St Mark, an ox for St Luke, and an eagle for St John. Above the door and below the dog-tooth band, the carved tympanum shows Christ in Glory, and below this is a carved tablet depicting the parable of the wise and foolish virgins. At the bottom are two small panels recording the murder of St Thomas Becket at Canterbury in 1170.

BRENTWOOD, HIGH STREET AND TOWN HALL 1895 35669

In 1805 a permanent army barracks was built at Warley, on the outskirts of Brentwood. The soldiers were sent out to fight in many different parts of the world, and in 1812 the 2nd Battalion 44th Foot was involved in the battle of Salamanca. They captured the French standard depicting an eagle, and this symbol was added to their badge. The battalion later became part of the Essex Regiment. Then in 1842 the East India Company bought the barracks. It was during their time that the garrison church was built; it is now known as the Essex Regiment Church, and the colours hanging in the church are a reminder of the many battles in which the regiment was engaged. The garrison was taken over by the War Office in 1861, and it played an active part in both the world wars of the 20th century. The barracks closed and most of the buildings were sold in the 1960s; however, the church remains, standing beside the old Barrack Road, which is now renamed Eagle Way after the eagle on the French standard captured at the battle of Salamanca.

North of Brentford, off the A128 Chipping Ongar to Brentwood road near the village of Kelvedon Hatch, is one of Britain's strangest and creepiest museums, The Kelvedon Hatch Secret Nuclear Bunker. It was built during the Cold War, the period after the Second World War when relations with Russia were strained, and was intended to be the place where the Prime Minister and up to 600 civilian and military personnel could take shelter in the event of atomic war breaking out, and from where they could continue to run the country. When the underground bunker was closed in 1992, the farmer whose land it was on bought it and turned it into a 40-roomed museum filled with artefacts from the Cold War period, including a BBC studio from which broadcasts would have been made to anyone surviving in the outside world.

In the feature film 'Four Weddings and a Funeral', the funeral takes place in a church in Essex – St Clement's Church in West Thurrock, near Grays.

The Thames estuary forms much of the southern border of Essex. The chalk outcrops along the estuary near Purfleet were formerly quarried for agricultural lime and 'whiting', but later produced quantities of cement. Samuel Whitbread purchased the chalk quarries and surrounding estate in the 1790s, and the Whitbread family went on to develop a planned village at Purfleet, much of which is now in the Purfleet Conservation Area. The first horse-drawn railway in Essex was used at Purfleet in 1803, in the chalk pits of the Whitbread Estate. Purfleet enjoyed a brief vogue among day trippers from London in the 19th century, and someone who seems to have visited at this time was Bram Stoker, author of the Gothic novel 'Dracula'. In this work, Count Dracula purchases a property known as 'Carfax' in Purfleet to use as a centre for his vampire activities. The connection is commemorated in Purfleet with a plaque on the wall of St Stephen's Church.

Brick- and tile-making, employing the fine wind-blown 'brick earth' of the Thames estuary around Grays, was once an important local industry that helped build Victorian London. Defoe Parade in Chadwell St Mary, just north of Grays, commemorates Daniel Defoe (c1660-1731), author of 'Robinson Crusoe', who lived in Chadwell in the 1690s and opened a tile factory in the parish. Unfortunately for him, the business failed.

Tilbury Docks – the lowest on the Thames – opened in 1886; they were purpose-built, to be deep enough for very large ships to enter or leave at high and low tide. Cargo boats have now been superseded by the rise of the container ship, and the Port of Tilbury is now one of the largest container ports in Europe.

In 1667 a Dutch invasion fleet paid a visit to the Essex coast. East Tilbury church got in the way of a stray cannonball and, to this day, has no tower.

The Bell Inn at Horndon on the Hill has unusual décor – every year since 1901, on Good Friday at Easter, a hot cross bun has been nailed to the rafters! The custom was started by Jack Turnell when he became the new landlord of the Bell, and has continued ever since. The tradition carried on even during the rationing years of the Second World War, but those wartime buns were made of concrete.

In past centuries, malaria inflicted misery on many villagers and marsh dwellers along the Essex coast. There are five indigenous species of Anopheles mosquito capable of transmitting malaria in England, and they were particularly prevalent in the past in the low-lying, undrained marshes of Essex and Kent, where fever, rheumatism and 'ague' (the local name for malaria) were very common. In 1722 Daniel Defoe wrote of his grand tour of Britain, which took him along the course of the A13. He was astounded at the death rate of the children and women on the marshland at Fobbing and Corringham. The men bred in this area were hardened to it, but went to the higher land to find their wives. Many of these women contracted the ague, and seldom lasted more than a year. For a man in the area to have sixteen wives was not exceptional, and one farmer in Canvey married twenty-five wives!

The Hoy & Helmet pub at South Benfleet was originally built in the 15th century, with later extensions. The 'hoy' of the pub's intriguing name was a broad, flat-bottomed sailing boat that was used to transport both cargo like farming produce and passengers along the coast and on the Thames; from this came the nautical cry of 'Ahoy', used to hail a hoy to stop and take on a passenger. The word 'helmet' was added to the name of the pub in 1922, this being the term for the hard on which the boats were drawn up.

The low-lying area of Canvey Island has been a great Thames-side attraction for many years, though now the sea walls have been raised to protect the region being inundated by the sea in the event of the closing of the Thames Barrier. In the terrible floods of January 1953, there were 58 deaths on Canvey Island and 35 at Jaywick, further up the low-lying Essex coast. It is an old problem – as early as the 1620s, a Dutch entrepreneur called Joas Croppenburg was called in to furnish Canvey with a serviceable sea wall. A number of Dutch settlers fleeing religious persecution came to this part of Essex in the 17th century; they helped build sea defences and reclaim several islands from the sea in return for farmland. These Dutch settlers built a number of tiny octagonal thatched cottages in the area, one of which is now the Dutch Cottage Museum on Canvey Road, which houses a variety of exhibits about the history of Canvey Island. It is thought that these cottages were built round because they were easier to thatch, and also perhaps because the round design did not leave any corners for evil spirits or the Devil to lurk in.

Rochford stands on the River Roach, a few miles north of Southend. On the outskirts of the town is Rochford Hall, possibly the birthplace c1504 of Anne Boleyn, the second wife of Henry VIII; it was certainly one of her childhood homes. The manor of Rochford was held by Anne's father, Sir Thomas Boleyn, who was created Viscount Rochford in 1525. It was around this time that his daughter caught the roving eye of the king, and the couple are reputed to have met at Rochford Hall in secret during their long courtship. Later, the Hall was the home of Anne's sister Mary and her second husband, William Stafford, Lord Chebsey, after their marriage in 1534. Rochford Hall, much altered since Anne Boleyn's day, is privately owned and not open to the public.

Before the seaside resort of Southend was developed, it was just a small area of fishermen's huts at the end of a lane south of Prittlewell – the original 'Southende'. By the middle of the 18th century it became fashionable to visit the seaside. It was thought that the sea air and water gave help to those with health problems, and in 1758 the Ship Inn was built at what is now Southend, the resort's first hotel. Fashionable visitors made the journey from London to Southend by horse-drawn coach or by the weekly packet boat. More accommodation was needed, and a grand hotel was built at New Southe-End, with two terraces of fine houses, at the top of what is now known as Pier Hill. Southend really took off with the coming of the railway in 1856 – visitors could now reach the town easily, stay for the day and return home at night – the time of the day-tripper had arrived. Queen Victoria signed the town's Charter of Incorporation in 1892, and at this point the town was officially named Southend-on-Sea.

**SOUTHEND
THE BOATING LAKE AND
PIER HILL c1950** S155020

SOUTHEND-ON-SEA, THE PIER 1898 41377

Southend has the longest iron pleasure pier in the world, reaching out 1.34 miles (2158m) into the Thames estuary. The pier was opened in 1889, replacing an earlier wooden pier, and its record-breaking extensions were added later. In 1890 a single-track electric railway began operating, which took people to the pier head – the first pier railway in the country. Various disasters have occurred to the pier over the years, including a number of fires and being crashed into by ships, but it remains a much-loved part of the resort. It was the favourite pier of Sir John Betjeman, first president of the National Piers Society, who said 'the Pier is Southend, Southend is the Pier'. Southend Pier Museum on Pier Hill has an excellent display of memorabilia and information on the history of this unique structure.

An annual event in Southend is the Whitebait Festival, which takes place in September. Whitebait are the tiny silver fry (young) of sprats or herrings, and are eaten whole, fried until crisp. The whitebait harvest was important to Southend in past years, and small quantities of this fish are still landed here. The Whitebait Festival begins with a special service at the end of Southend Pier to bless the first catch of the season.

Basildon has an interesting history, for it was 'reinvented' not once, but twice. At the start of the 19th century Basildon was a small rural parish, bounded on the west by Laindon, Dunton, Langdon Hills and Lee Chapel, and on the south and east by Vange, Pitsea and Nevendon. They were quiet, agricultural places – but an agricultural depression in the 1870s caused landowners to look for new uses for their land. Land-agents began to acquire land in the area, carving it into small plots, roughly 18ft wide, and offering them for sale as cheap building plots. Thousands of people eventually bought plots, and bizarre townships of shacks and bungalows sprouted up, particularly during the 1920s and 30s, as many people welcomed the chance to build their own home at a low cost. The estates lacked many basic amenities though: mains water was out of the question for most plotland dwellings, and many roads were just grass tracks, almost impassable in winter. By 1940 the population of Laindon-Pitsea was 25,000. The local authority, Billericay Urban District Council, was concerned about the lack of facilities in the area, but could not afford to give this huge sprawling settlement the makeover it needed. However, when the New Towns Act was passed in 1946 and the search began for locations to re-house thousands of Londoners who had lost their homes during the Second World War, Billericay UDC grasped the opportunity to re-plan and rebuild the settlement on a major scale, and was unique in actually asking to be considered as the site for a New Town. The scheme was given official approval in 1948. Although some residents of the plotlands welcomed the New Town with open arms, delighted at the prospect of new homes with electric lighting, brick walls and flushing toilets, many others were not happy; for years, they had poured all their hopes, resources and time into what was now being described as a 'shanty town'. Some plotlanders barricaded themselves inside their homes, or even clambered onto their roofs with shotguns to resist the loss of their homes. 'Basildon was built on tears' became a familiar observation.

The Development Corporation at Basildon spent the next 37 years building homes for up to 50,000 people in the 'New Town', in 15 self-contained 'neighbourhoods'. An area between Laindon and Pitsea, not far from the old village of Basildon, had been selected as the centre of the New Town and the state-of-the-art market place opened in 1958, designed in the stark angularity favoured by architects of the period, intent on constructing a 'brave new world'. Maurice Lambert's 'Mother and Child' statue was commissioned for Basildon's Town Square in 1959, as a symbol of the New Town's growth. The statue now forms part of Basildon's logo, such has been the extent to which people associate it with the town.

Honeypot Lane is a famous old Basildon road name that has survived the building of the new town. It once ran from Clay Hill Road to Pipps Hill Road, and is called Honeypot Lane because the sticky yellow clay of the area made the road impassable in winter.

BASILDON, TOWN SQUARE, THE 'MOTHER AND CHILD' STATUE 1961 B43800l

Soon after the Roman conquest of Britain in the first century AD, a Roman encampment was established at the point where the Roman road from London to Colchester bridged the River Can. After a while, it developed into a small town called 'Caesaromagus' ('Caesar's plain') – the only town in Britain to bear Caesar's name. Everything had crumbled away, however, by the time the Saxons arrived – even the bridge. The new settlers avoided settling on the old site, preferring the higher ground near what is now Rectory Lane. Nevertheless, there was one particular East Saxon – a man called Ceolmaer – who was in some way connected with a ford across the smaller of the two local rivers, and gave his name to it: Ceolmaer's ford, which became 'Chelmsford', although there was no town there at that time. Chelmsford, as we know it, was founded in 1199 by William of Sainte-Mère-Église, Bishop of London. In that year, King John granted him the right to hold a market once a week on the lane that is now the High Street. He divided the land on either side of the lane into plots that people could purchase as freeholds. Situated on the main road from London to Colchester, Chelmsford was ideally placed for such an enterprise. A triangular market place appeared, the market-stalls became permanent shops, and a church was built to serve the new community. Chelmsford made a good stop-over point for courtiers on royal business; its central position meant it was a convenient place for Essex's assizes to be held; and by the mid 13th century, Chelmsford had become the county town, which it still remains.

In 1988, the Roman town of 'Caesaromagus' was the setting for a BBC TV sitcom, 'Chelmsford 123' which was set in the town in the year AD 123. The show concerned the attempts of the ineffectual Roman governor Aulus Paulinus to subdue Badvoc, the unruly leader of the local tribesmen. The main characters – wholly fictitious – were played by Jimmy Mulville and Rory McGrath, who also wrote the series. It ran for two seasons.

Tindal Square in Chelmsford is dominated by the Shire Hall, built between 1789 and 1791. The three panels beneath the pediment on the front of the Shire Hall represent Wisdom, Mercy and Justice. Tindal Square and Tindal Street in Chelmsford are named after Sir Nicholas Conyngham Tindal (1776-1846), Chief Justice of Common Pleas, who was born in 1776 in Moulsham Street and educated at the Grammar School. One of Chelmsford's most famous sons, a statue of him stands in Tindal Square. Judge Tindal was responsible for two significant legal rulings: one was the inception of the special verdict of 'Not Guilty by reason of insanity' at the trial of Daniel M'Naughten (known as 'the M'Naughten Rules'), and the other was in the case of Regina v Hale, when he ruled that where a defendant was provoked to such an unreasonable degree that he lost his self-control and killed the person responsible for that provocation, the defendant would be guilty of manslaughter, not murder. Tindal's reforms to the application of the criminal law, recognising the importance of differing states of mind *(mens rea)* with regard to vulnerable prisoners accused of serious crimes, were social reforms of great importance.

CHELMSFORD, THE SHIRE HALL 1892 31507

Guglielmo Marconi arrived in Chelmsford in 1898 at the age of 22. He was fascinated by electromagnetic waves, especially as a means of communication, and took over a disused silk-factory in Hall Street which he turned into the Wireless, Telegraph and Signal Company Ltd, the world's first radio factory. Within a decade he had established radio links with continental Europe and the United States, and scooped up a Nobel Prize for Physics. By 1912 the Hall Street site was too small, and a new works was built in New Street. Britain's first publicised broadcast of entertainment was a performance by the Australian soprano Dame Nellie Melba, which was transmitted in 1920 from Marconi's New Street works. Dame Nellie sang into a microphone that had been cobbled together from a telephone receiver and a cigar box, which is preserved in the Marconi collection of the Museum of the History of Science at Oxford. Capitalising on the success of this performance, the Marconi company set up a regular radio station in an ex-army hut at Writtle. It stood just off Lawford Lane. The hut – known by its call sign, Two Emma Toc – is now preserved in the industrial heritage centre at Sandford Mill. Its original site is now a housing development, Melba Court.

Chelmsford Cathedral was simply St Mary's parish church until 1914, when it achieved new status as a cathedral at the hub of England's largest diocese. The cathedral's original dedication was expanded to St Mary, St Peter and St Cedd in 1954. The last-named was the Northumbrian cleric who had introduced Christianity to the East Saxons some 1,300 years earlier. On the exterior of the cathedral is a carved figure of St Peter dressed in the clothes of a modern-day fisherman, including a wool hat and wellies, and carrying the Key of Heaven – in the form of a Yale key.

One of Chelmsford's strangest curiosities must be the area of Writtle Road cemetery reserved for the graves of travelling showmen. Displaying a robust attitude to the afterlife, the graves are adorned with gilded, marble pick-up trucks, or etched with representations fairground attractions such as ferris-wheels and helter-skelters.

CHELMSFORD, THE CATHEDRAL, THE ST PETER STATUE
2005 C73717

Maldon is situated on the River Blackwater, one of the saltiest rivers in England. A crystal sea salt, which has a more pronounced flavour than ordinary salt, has been produced there for many centuries. Maldon was once full of flourmills, maltings, ropewalks and boatyards. It was a significant port too, handling corn, coal, chalk and hay. These goods were transported, as were other Essex commodities along the coast such as bricks and lime, by the Thames sailing barge. These superb boats with their big tan sails were generally worked all along the Essex coast to the Thames estuary. With their flat bottoms they could be run up on a beach at low tide, their cargoes unloaded, and then floated off on the high tide. Part of the surviving fleet of Thames barges has now been converted to pleasure use and is based at Maldon, which had been a sailing barge centre for many years; many barges were built here, especially at Cook's Yard, which later maintained the local trading barge fleet.

Tollesbury is a large maritime village, known for its oysters, on the northern side of the Blackwater estuary. It is also famous for the font in the parish church of St Mary, which bears a unique inscription urging the congregation not to swear: 'Good people all I pray take care that in ye Church you doe not sware As this man did.' The font, and the inscription, was paid for in 1718 by the churchwardens with the proceeds of a fine they had demanded from one John Norman. According to the church register for 30th August 1817, he 'came drunk into ye Church and cursed and talked aloud in the time of Divine Service, to prevent his being prosecuted for which he paid by agreement the above said five pounds'. The entry also record that 'the wise Rhyms on the font were put there by sole order of Robert Joyce then Church Warden'.

BRAINTREE, HIGH STREET 1906 55533

Braintree developed around the crossing point of east-west and north-south roads on the important pilgrimage routes to Bury St Edmunds in Suffolk and Walsingham in Norfolk. From the 15th century onwards a flourishing woollen industry developed in the town, first producing heavy broadcloth, and later the light cloth which took its name from neighbouring Bocking; this industry was a major factor in the prosperity of the town for around 400 years. As the 19th century dawned, the wool industry had ceased and the silk industry had taken its place. The Courtaulds silk mills in Braintree once employed over 3,000 local people. Warner & Son supplied the silk used in various royal ceremonies for George VI, Elizabeth II and the Prince of Wales, as well as velvet for all the coronations between that of Edward VII in 1902 and Elizabeth II in 1953. Warners ceased weaving in Braintree in 1971 but some of the old hand looms were rescued and can be seen in use at The Working Silk Museum in New Mills in South Street.

The modern town of Colchester stands on ancient foundations, and is claimed to be 'Britain's Oldest Recorded Town'. The street plan of medieval Colchester survives virtually intact in the layout of the present-day town, and much of this was based on the Roman town laid out beneath it in the first century AD. At the time of the Roman invasion of Britain in AD43, a Celtic town stood where Colchester is now, the capital of the powerful Catuvellauni tribe. The Romans Latinised the Celtic name of the town, calling it 'Camulodunum' – Camulos was a Celtic war god, and 'dunum' is from the Celtic word 'dun', for fort. In the early stages of the Roman conquest of Britain the Emperor Claudius himself came to Camulodunum, where he received the surrender of native tribes. His triumphal entry into the town included war elephants. By around AD50, Camulodunum had become a 'colonia', or settlement for retired legionaries, and was the most important town in the Roman province of Britannia. When Boudica, Queen of the Iceni tribe (in the Norfolk/Suffolk area), rose in revolt against the Romans around AD61, Camulodunum was one of her main targets, and the town was attacked and burned to the ground. After the defeat of Boudica's forces, Camulodunum was rebuilt, and re-walled in stone. It remained a prosperous town for the rest of the Roman period, but the up-and-coming port of London soon outstripped it as the premier settlement of Roman Britannia. There are still many visible remains of the Roman walls in present-day Colchester, as well as the Balkerne Gate. This was the great west gate, the entry to the Roman town from the London road and the grandest of all of the town's entrances. The importance of this west gate was emphasised by a stone-faced triumphal arch with the vehicle carriageways, each 17ft wide. The rest of the gate had a pedestrian way each side and a quadrant bastion, which contained a north and south guardroom. Much of it survives today, including the south pedestrian way (still in use), and its guardroom bastion. The north bastion, pedestrian way and parts of the triumphal arch foundations remain under (and supporting) the Hole in the Wall pub on Balkerne Hill.

COLCHESTER, HIGH STREET 1902 48299

After the Romans left Britain in the early 5th century the Saxons occupied the town of Camulodonum and gave it their own name, 'Colne Caester', which means 'the Roman fortress on the River Colne'. Local legend in the past associated the name of Colchester with the legendary British king, 'Old King Cole', the 'merry old soul' of the popular rhyme, and claimed that his daughter Helena was the mother of Constantine the Great (AD306-337), the first Christian Roman Emperor, who made Christianity the official religion of the Roman Empire. Although the story about Old King Cole is unlikely to be true, St Helena remains the patron saint of Colchester, and there is a bronze statue of her atop Colchester's wonderfully over-the-top Baroque town hall, seen in the photograph above. In the background of this photograph is the huge water tower that still stands in Colchester. It is locally known as Jumbo, because this 105ft tower was built in 1882 – the same year that a famous elephant called Jumbo had arrived at London Zoo.

In the late 16th century Protestant refugees from the Spanish Netherlands (now Belgium) arrived in Colchester. These latter-day asylum seekers were skilled weavers and revitalised Colchester's cloth industry. They settled in the part of town known as the Dutch Quarter, north of the High Street, in areas such as West Stockwell Street, where they made the type of cloth called 'bays', or baize.

A plaque on a house in West Stockwell Street records that it was the home from 1796 to 1811 of sisters Jane and Ann Taylor, writers of children's verses. Jane Taylor's name may not be familiar to many people nowadays, but her most famous poem will be – 'Twinkle, Twinkle, Little Star'.

Colchester sided with Parliament in the Civil War, but in 1648 a Royalist force seized the town. A bloody siege followed, and after eleven weeks of bombardment and fighting, the town fell. Much damage was done to the town during this siege. Some of the town walls and many houses were reduced to rubble, and all but the base of the tower of the church of St-Mary-at-the-Walls was destroyed – the tower was being used by Royalist snipers, and this attracted Parliamentary cannon fire. There is a theory that the nursery rhyme 'Humpty Dumpty' recalls the bombardment of the church, with 'Humpty Dumpty' referring to a portly Royalist sniper called One-Eyed Thomson, who was positioned in the belfry of the church, 'sat on the wall'; when he was shot down he 'had a great fall'; and 'all the king's horses and all the king's men' refers to the Royalist forces. Another theory is that 'Humpty Dumpty' was the nickname of a Royalist cannon positioned at the top of the tower, which was knocked down by Parliamentary cannonballs.

Colchester has been at the heart of the oyster trade in Britain for many years, and the oyster season is opened by a traditional festival in early September. The Mayor, civic dignitaries and members of the Fishing Board go by boat to Pyfleet Creek, where the oyster fattening beds lie. Here the loyal toast is drunk, gingerbread and gin are consumed, and the Mayor makes the first ceremonial oyster dredge of the season. The town also holds an annual Oyster Feast in October.

LAYER MARNEY, THE TOWER 1892 31548

A few miles south-west of Colchester, the magnificent eight-storey gatehouse of Layer Marney Tower was built by Sir Henry, 1st Lord Marney, around 1520 and is the tallest Tudor gateway in England. The rest of the mansion he had planned was never built; Sir Henry died in 1523 and the Marneys were extinct two years later. All that remains of Sir Henry's grandiose plan is this gatehouse, renowned for its sheer scale, and for the terracotta ornamentation on the parapets. Layer Marney Tower and gardens are open to the public from March to October. The gardens are Grade II listed on the English Heritage Register of Parks and Gardens of Special Historic Interest in England.

To the east of Colchester, at Elmstead (sometimes called Elmstead Market), are the Beth Chatto Gardens. These were created out of wasteland and feature three distinct areas, a dry, a shaded and a wetland garden, each with their own distinct planting scheme, featuring over 1,000 species in all.

Brightlingsea is south of Colchester on the Colne estuary. Largely concerned with oysters and sprat fishing, the parish is technically an island – that is what the '-ea' in its name means. Famous for its boatyards, which still produce yachts and ships, Brightlingsea is a 'limb' of the Cinque Port of Sandwich in Kent, and each December a Deputy of the Cinque Port Liberty is elected in the town to swear allegiance to the mayor of Sandwich. In All Saints' Parish Church at Brightlingsea there are more than 200 memorial plaques, each one to a local person lost at sea; this was the idea of a 19th-century vicar, the Rev Andrew Pertwee, who also used to stand on the parapet of the flint church tower with a lantern at night, hoping to guide seafarers safely home.

The rich Essex farmland, famed for its wheat, and the many rivers, creeks and tidal inlets, combined to make ideal locations for big corn mills in the past. These were no local mills, catering for the immediate community, but industrial-scale establishments. Some were ordinary water mills, but many were tide mills. The only remaining tide mill in Essex is at Thorrington, a short distance north of Brightlinsea, standing where the Tenpenny Brook flows into the Alresford Creek, a tributary of the River Colne.

Previously known as Chich, the isolated village of St Osyth (generally pronounced 'Toosey') between Brightlingsea and Clacton-on-Sea takes its name from Osyth, an East Anglian princess who was the daughter of the first East Anglian Christian king. She established a nunnery here, but in AD653 it was sacked by the Danes and Osyth was beheaded. A holy well is said to have gushed forth where her head hit the ground. St Osyth's Priory, founded as an Augustinian house in 1118, supposedly occupies the former site of St Osyth's nunnery. The magnificent 15th-century flint-decorated gatehouse of the priory is one of the finest monastic buildings in the country (see photograph 35701, opposite).

During the Napoleonic Wars (1803-15) several Martello towers were installed on the Essex coast to protect the shoreline of the Tendring peninsula. These squat, round towers with extra thick walls on the seaward side were inspired by a fortification at Mortella Point in Corsica. The Martello tower at Point Clear at St Osyth now houses the museum of the East Essex Aviation Society. Pride of place in the museum is taken by the remains of a crashed American P51 Mustang of the US 479th Fighter Group that ditched into the sea off Clacton in 1945, as well as a memorial display to the pilot, who sadly died after being rescued from the sea. The museum also holds a large collection of exhibits covering the major conflicts of this century, including an extensive model collection and various memorabilia from the First World War, the Second World War, Army, Navy and American Forces, the Home Front, Civil Defence and Observation Corps, and much more. Another Martello tower in the area is on the Promenade at Jaywick; it has been beautifully renovated, and is now used as an art, heritage and community venue.

ST OSYTH, THE PRIORY GATEHOUSE 1895 35701

CLACTON-ON-SEA, THE PIER 1907 58929

Until the second half of the 19th century, Clacton-on-Sea did not exist. What is now the centre of the town was a desolate part of the coast known as Clacton Beach, after the village of Great Clacton a mile or so inland. In the 1860s the land that became the centre of Clacton-on-Sea was bought by Peter Bruff, the engineer on the Colchester to Walton railway that was then being built. Bruff intented to turn the area into a seaside resort as a speculative business venture, and it is from this date that the real history of Clacton-on-Sea begins. In 1866 Bruff was granted Parliamentary powers to construct a branch line from his railway to Clacton and to build a pier. In return for the rights to operate his company's steamers to and from the pier, William Parry Jackson, the chairman of the Woolwich Steam Packet Company, agreed to finance Bruff's scheme. The first steamer to call at the pier was the 'Queen of the Orwell', which called in on its way to Ipswich on 18th July 1871, a date which could be said to be the birth of Clacton-on-Sea.

Having built the pier, the next move by Peter Bruff and the directors of the Woolwich Steam Packet Company was to build the Royal Hotel, which opened in 1872. Peter Bruff then began to sell off plots of land around Pier Avenue to developers, but he laid down very strict conditions dealing with draining, fencing, paving, lighting and other improvements. It is largely due to Bruff that the centre of Clacton still retains its airy and well-laid out feel with wide streets and well-spaced shops and houses. In 1877 the directors of the Woolwich Steam Packet Company, many of whom – such as Jackson, Ellis, Hayes, Penfold and Agate – are remembered by roads named after them in the centre of town, bought up all the unsold plots of land from Bruff and set about developing Clacton. The photograph below shows Electric Parade in Clacton in 1913, so-called because it was the first part of Clacton to be lit by electricity (in 1901). The name Electric Parade was discontinued at the end of the 1950s and the shops along it were renumbered as part of Pier Avenue.

CLACTON-ON-SEA, ELECTRIC PARADE 1913 65239

HARWICH, THE QUAYSIDE c1954 HI50006

Harwich is arguably the finest medieval town in Essex. It was
developed on a grid pattern in the 13th century by the Earl of Norfolk
who saw the potential of its position at the mouth of the Stour and
Orwell estuaries. It soon became an important port and harbour,
and in the 17th century it was the headquarters of the King's Navy.
Harwich still retains a wealth of historic buildings, and the Maritime
Heritage Trail commemorates the town's long connection with the
sea. One of the interesting sights to be seen in the town is the old
treadmill crane which originally stood in Harwich's old shipyard but
has been painstakingly restored and now stands on Harwich Green,
by the town's eastern shoreline. This 17th-century timber device was
used to shift cargo and ships' parts. It looks like a modern crane, with
a jib from which a retractable hook hangs down, which juts out from
a wooden hut that houses two large wheels. The crane was powered
by two men working inside these wheels, pedalling away madly like
hamsters whilst instructions were shouted to them from outside.

Essex has the unhappy distinction of having executed more witches than any other county in England's history, and the first major trial for witchcraft itself, as the main indictment, took place in Chelmsford in 1566 when 63-year-old Agnes Waterhouse of Hatfield Peverell was found guilty and hanged. One of the most unpleasant characters in the county's story was Matthew Hopkins, who lived at Manningtree in north-east Essex in the mid 17th century. After denouncing his crippled neighbour as a witch, Hopkins realised he had a particular talent for terrorising old women that could make him powerful and wealthy. He claimed to hold the 'Devil's own list of all the witches in England', and as the hysteria of witch-fever gripped East Anglia in 1645-46, many towns paid him to come and search for 'witches'. He assumed the title of 'Witchfinder General', made his headquarters in Colchester, and is believed to have been responsible for the deaths of up to 400 people throughout East Anglia; people were either denounced by neighbours (who were rewarded for the information) or tortured until they confessed, and were put to death for witchcraft on the most flimsy evidence. His reign of terror at last came to an end when John Gaule, a Huntingdonshire parson, decided that enough was enough and it was time Hopkins received his come-uppance. He preached a number of scathing sermons denouncing Hopkins and published his sermons in a pamphlet in which he attacked Hopkins and his accomplices, particularly denouncing his methods of obtaining 'confessions' by means of torture which, as he pointed out, was actually illegal in England at that time. His complaints helped lead to Hopkins being formally questioned about his methods, after which he retired from witch hunting and went home to Manningtree, where he died soon after, probably in 1647. He was buried at Mistley Heath, but that isn't the last of the story – his ghost is said to haunt the area around Mistley pond, particularly at the time of the full moon…

SPORTING ESSEX

A cricketing resident of Old Harlow in the 19th century was a local businessman called Samuel Deards. Becoming irritated by the method of scoring, he invented the type of scoreboard used everywhere nowadays. Harlow Cricket Club, which plays at its Old Harlow ground of 'Marigolds', was the site of the world's first mechanical cricket scoreboard.

The earliest recorded reference to a county cricket team from Essex was in July 1732, when a combined Essex & Hertfordshire team played against the famous London Cricket Club 'for £50 a side, play or pay; wickets to be pitched at one o'clock precisely or forfeit half the money'. The present-day Essex County Cricket Club plays most of its home games at the County Cricket Ground at Chelsmford, but also plays at Lower Castle Park in Colchester and Garons Park at Southend. Its limited overs team, the Essex Eagles, won the National League in 2005 and 2006 and the Friends Provident Trophy in 2008. To date (2011) Essex County Cricket Club has won the County Championship 6 times, in 1979, 1983, 1984, 1986, 1991 and 1992. A great name in Essex Cricket Club's history is Graham Gooch, OBE, DL (born 1953), who played for the county between 1973 and 1997, and captained both Essex and England. Through a career spanning from 1973 until 2000, he became the most prolific run scorer of all time with 67,057 runs. He currently (2011) holds the record as the leading Test run scorer for England, and is one of only twenty-five players to have scored over 100 first-class centuries. Another famous name in the club is Alastair Cook (born 1984), a left-handed opening batsman who currently (2011) plays county cricket for Essex and Test cricket for England. Cook played for Essex's Academy and made his debut for the first XI in 2003. He played a pivotal role in retaining the 2010-11 Ashes series in Australia, breaking records by scoring the second highest number of runs in a Test series by Englishman.

Essex has two football teams in the Football League, Colchester United FC and Southend United FC. Colchester United Football Club, nicknamed 'The Oystermen', were responsible for one of the greatest upsets in the history of the FA Cup when in 1971 they beat the all-conquering Leeds United 3-2 at Layer Road; their victory caused Colchester United to be the first League team to be mentioned in Hansards, the Parliamentary minutes. Southend United Football Club, known variously as The Shrimpers, The Seasiders and The Blues, was formed in 1906 and elected to the Football League in 1920 – a highlight of that season was a 4-1 victory over Spurs in the 4th round of the FA Cup. There is great rivalry between Southend United and Colchester United, and the two clubs contest the Essex derby. The record currently stands at 29 wins to Southend, 23 wins for Colchester and 17 draws (as at 2011).

Burnham-on-Crouch is a major yachting centre, and hosts a sailing event known as 'Burnham Week' every August, a week of competitive yacht and dinghy racing on the River Crouch that is shared by the The Royal Corinthian Yacht Club, The Royal Burnham Yacht Club, The Crouch Yacht Club, and The Burnham Sailing Club.

BURNHAM-ON-CROUCH, THE RIVER c1965 B325129

47

QUIZ QUESTIONS

Answers on page 52.

1. What is the traditional nickname for a person from Essex?

2. Which of William Shakespeare's plays is about an ancient British king who ruled in the Essex area in the years just before the Roman conquest in AD43?

3. What is the origin of the Essex phrase 'a Coggeshall job?'

4. Whereabouts in Essex will you find Wallace the lion, and how did he become famous?

5. Why was Essex 'all shook up' in 1884?

6. What is The Essex Way?

7. What terrifying event happened at Southend in May 1915?

8. The 16th-century timber-framed Chantry Café building in Billericay seen in the 1950's photograph B319013 (opposite) is now known as Chantry House. The building has an important place in the history of the USA – why?

9. In December 2004 archaeologists working on a housing development at Colchester unearthed what they believe is almost certainly the only known Roman circus in Britain. The site was the subject of a special 'Time Team' TV programme in May 2005. A circus was the largest entertainment building in the Roman world, and Colchester's was about 70 metres wide and 350 metres long – but what was it used for?

10. What is known in Essex as a 'pagle'? (Also spelled as 'paigle' or 'peggle'.)

BILLERICAY, THE CHANTRY CAFÉ c1955 B319013

RECIPE

ESSEX PEA SOUP

Pea pods have an intense flavour, and this traditional recipe from Essex ensures that this is not wasted. For a true flavour of Essex, why not use Kelvedon Wonder peas – this variety of pea was developed in Essex in 1925. It is a popular dwarf variety for spring sowing, and very good for summer sowing to produce a later crop, and yields well filled, dark green, pointed pods and peas of outstandingly good flavour.

        450g/1 lb fresh peas in their pods
        1 onion
        50g/2oz butter
        900ml/1½ pints good ham or vegetable stock
        1 teaspoonful of sugar
        2 sprigs of fresh mint
        1 teaspoonful of cornflour
        300ml/ ½ pint milk
        Salt and pepper

Shell the peas, wash the empty pods and remove the stringy edge and any other hard, fibrous bits. Peel and finely chop the onion. Melt the butter in a large heavy saucepan, add the peas, pods and chopped onion and fry gently for a few minutes until softened. Add the stock, sugar and sprigs of mint. Bring to the boil, then reduce heat, cover and simmer until the peas and pods are tender. Blend the cornflour with a little milk and stir it into the soup, together with the remaining milk. Increase the heat and bring the soup back to the boil, stirring all the time. Remove from heat and allow to it cool for a few minutes, then liquidise the soup in a blender or pass it through a sieve. Season the soup with salt and pepper to taste, and reheat before serving.

RECIPE

ESSEX SPICE CAKES

These are more like large biscuits than cakes, and were probably originally made at the time of religious festivals. Rosewater was commonly used in English cookery in the past. It is available from specialist cookshops, or selected stores of larger supermarkets – one brand to look out for is English Provender rosewater.

> 225g/8oz caster sugar
> 175g/6oz butter or margarine, softened
> 2 eggs, beaten
> 1 teaspoonful rosewater
> 225g/8oz plain flour
> 1 teaspoonful baking powder
> A pinch of salt
> A pinch of ground mace
> A pinch of ground cloves (or allspice)
> Half a teaspoonful ground cinnamon
> 115g/4oz currants

Pre-heat the oven to 190°C/375°F/Gas Mark 5, and grease a baking tray.

Cream together the butter and sugar in a large bowl until the mixture is light and fluffy. Gradually mix in the beaten egg and rosewater, a little at a time, adding in a little of the flour if necessary to ensure the mixture does not curdle. Sift in the flour, baking powder, salt and spices and use a large metal spoon to fold it all into the mixture thoroughly, then fold in the currants. Place dessertspoonfuls of the mixture on the greased baking tray, making sure they are spaced well apart as they will spread during cooking. Bake in the pre-heated oven for 10-15 minutes. When cooked, allow to cool on the tray slightly, then remove with a palette knife and transfer to a wire tray to cool. Store in an airtight container.

QUIZ ANSWERS

1. The traditional nickname for a person from Essex is an Essex Calf, because the county used to be famous for the beef cattle and large calves that were reared there for the London meat markets.

2. Shakespeare's play 'Cymbeline' is about Cunobelinus, the powerful king of the Celtic Catuvellauni tribe of what is now Essex, who ruled from approximately AD7-40, just before the Roman invasion of Britain in AD43. The chief settlement of the Catuvellauni was at what is now Colchester. Under Cunobelinus's leadership, the Catuvellauni overran the territory of the neighbouring Trinovantes and conquered the area now known as Kent. By the end of his life Cunobelinus controlled most of south-east Britain, and the Roman historian Suetonius called him 'the king of the Britons'.

3. The Essex phrase 'a Coggeshall Job', which is used to describe a foolish piece of work, is said to have originated in several ways. One version says that one day Coggeshall's town clock struck eleven times instead of twelve times at noon. When news came that the clock at Lexdon, near Colchester, had given an extra chime and struck twelve times at eleven o'clock, a Coggeshall man reputedly set off with a horse and trap to bring back the missing stroke. Another version says that some Coggleshall people tried to divert the current of a local stream by fixing a hurdle in its bed, and yet another says that when a mad dog bit a wheelbarrow the local people feared that the barrow would catch the madness, and chained it up in a shed.

4. Wallace the lion is in Saffron Walden's museum, housed in what was one of the earliest purpose-built museums in the country when it opened in 1835. Wallace was the first lion to be bred in Britain and was a star of George Wombwell's 19th-century travelling menagerie of exotic beasts and birds. He was the inspiration for the lion in Marriott Edgar's poem 'Albert and the Lion' which was later adapted by Stanley Holloway as a comic monologue about young Albert who was eaten by the menagerie lion after pushing a stick into the unfortunate creature's ear to

liven him up a bit. After Wallace's death in 1838, his body was sent to the Saffron Walden museum to be stuffed and displayed in the natural history collection.

5. On the morning of 22nd April 1884, Essex was shaken by the strongest recorded earthquake to have struck England's mainland. The Great Essex Earthquake only lasted 20 seconds but was estimated to have destroyed 1,200 buildings in the area of Colchester and the surrounding villages, and many churches were damaged. The epicentre of the earthquake was in Colchester/ Wivenhoe area, and shockwaves were felt as far away as France and Belgium. Many ships and boats were also lost at sea in the giant waves that were caused by the tremors.

6. The Essex Way is a long-distance path across the county from Epping in the south-west to Harwich in the north-east. It covers a distance of 81 miles, mainly following footpaths and ancient green lanes.

7. In May 1915, during the First World War, Southend suffered an aerial bombardment when bombs were dropped on the town by hand from the giant Zeppelin airship LZ37.

8. Chantry House in Billericay is believed to have been the home of Christopher Martin, who was responsible for provisioning the 'Mayflower', the ship that carried the Pilgrim Fathers to America in 1620. Christopher Martin himself sailed on the 'Speedwell', the sister ship of the 'Mayflower', and was elected governor of the ship for the voyage. The 'Speedwell' developed leaks and turned back to England, but Christopher Martin and his family transferred to the 'Mayflower' and continued to America. Sadly, Christopher Martin, his wife and step-son all died in the first winter in their new land.

9. A Roman circus was a chariot-racing circuit.

10. 'Pagle' is the Essex name for a cowslip (primula veris). It is the traditional county flower of Essex. Paglesham is named after the flower, which is why it appears on the village sign.

FRANCIS FRITH

PIONEER VICTORIAN PHOTOGRAPHER

Francis Frith, founder of the world-famous photographic archive, was a complex and multi-talented man. A devout Quaker and a highly successful Victorian businessman, he was philosophical by nature and pioneering in outlook. By 1855 he had already established a wholesale grocery business in Liverpool, and sold it for the astonishing sum of £200,000, which is the equivalent today of over £15,000,000. Now in his thirties, and captivated by the new science of photography, Frith set out on a series of pioneering journeys up the Nile and to the Near East.

INTRIGUE AND EXPLORATION

He was the first photographer to venture beyond the sixth cataract of the Nile. Africa was still the mysterious 'Dark Continent', and Stanley and Livingstone's historic meeting was a decade into the future. The conditions for picture taking confound belief. He laboured for hours in his wicker dark-room in the sweltering heat of the desert, while the volatile chemicals fizzed dangerously in their trays. Back in London he exhibited his photographs and was 'rapturously cheered' by members of the Royal Society. His reputation as a photographer was made overnight.

VENTURE OF A LIFE-TIME

By the 1870s the railways had threaded their way across the country, and Bank Holidays and half-day Saturdays had been made obligatory by Act of Parliament. All of a sudden the working man and his family were able to enjoy days out, take holidays, and see a little more of the world.

With typical business acumen, Francis Frith foresaw that these new tourists would enjoy having souvenirs to commemorate their days out. For the next thirty years he travelled the country by train and by pony and trap, producing fine photographs of seaside resorts and beauty spots that were keenly bought by millions of Victorians. These prints were painstakingly pasted into family albums and pored over during the dark nights of winter, rekindling precious memories of summer excursions. Frith's studio was soon supplying retail shops all over the country, and by 1890 F Frith & Co had become the greatest specialist photographic publishing company in the world, with over 2,000 sales outlets, and pioneered the picture postcard.

FRANCIS FRITH'S LEGACY

Francis Frith had died in 1898 at his villa in Cannes, his great project still growing. By 1970 the archive he created contained over a third of a million pictures showing 7,000 British towns and villages.

Frith's legacy to us today is of immense significance and value, for the magnificent archive of evocative photographs he created provides a unique record of change in the cities, towns and villages throughout Britain over a century and more. Frith and his fellow studio photographers revisited locations many times down the years to update their views, compiling for us an enthralling and colourful pageant of British life and character.

We are fortunate that Frith was dedicated to recording the minutiae of everyday life. For it is this sheer wealth of visual data, the painstaking chronicle of changes in dress, transport, street layouts, buildings, housing and landscape that captivates us so much today, offering us a powerful link with the past and with the lives of our ancestors.

Computers have now made it possible for Frith's many thousands of images to be accessed almost instantly. The archive offers every one of us an opportunity to examine the places where we and our families have lived and worked down the years. Its images, depicting our shared past, are now bringing pleasure and enlightenment to millions around the world a century and more after his death.

For further information visit: www.francisfrith.com

INTERIOR DECORATION

Frith's photographs can be seen framed and as giant wall murals in thousands of pubs, restaurants, hotels, banks, retail stores and other public buildings throughout Britain. These provide interesting and attractive décor, generating strong local interest and acting as a powerful reminder of gentler days in our increasingly busy and frenetic world.

FRITH PRODUCTS

All Frith photographs are available as prints and posters in a variety of different sizes and styles. In the UK we also offer a range of other gift and stationery products illustrated with Frith photographs, although many of these are not available for delivery outside the UK – see our web site for more information on the products available for delivery in your country.

THE INTERNET

Over 100,000 photographs of Britain can be viewed and purchased on the Frith web site. The web site also includes memories and reminiscences contributed by our customers, who have personal knowledge of localities and of the people and properties depicted in Frith photographs. If you wish to learn more about a specific town or village you may find these reminiscences fascinating to browse. Why not add your own comments if you think they would be of interest to others? See **www.francisfrith.com**

PLEASE HELP US BRING FRITH'S PHOTOGRAPHS TO LIFE

Our authors do their best to recount the history of the places they write about. They give insights into how particular towns and villages developed, they describe the architecture of streets and buildings, and they discuss the lives of famous people who lived there. But however knowledgeable our authors are, the story they tell is necessarily incomplete.

Frith's photographs are so much more than plain historical documents. They are living proofs of the flow of human life down the generations. They show real people at real moments in history; and each of those people is the son or daughter of someone, the brother or sister, aunt or uncle, grandfather or grandmother of someone else. All of them lived, worked and played in the streets depicted in Frith's photographs.

We would be grateful if you would give us your insights into the places shown in our photographs: the streets and buildings, the shops, businesses and industries. Post your memories of life in those streets on the Frith website: what it was like growing up there, who ran the local shop and what shopping was like years ago; if your workplace is shown tell us about your working day and what the building is used for now. Read other visitors' memories and reconnect with your shared local history and heritage. With your help more and more Frith photographs can be brought to life, and vital memories preserved for posterity, and for the benefit of historians in the future.

Wherever possible, we will try to include some of your comments in future editions of our books. Moreover, if you spot errors in dates, titles or other facts, please let us know, because our archive records are not always completely accurate—they rely on 140 years of human endeavour and hand-compiled records. You can email us using the contact form on the website.

Thank you!

For further information, trade, or author enquiries
please contact us at the address below:

**The Francis Frith Collection, Unit 6, Oakley Business Park,
Wylye Road, Dinton, Wiltshire SP3 5EU.**
Tel: +44 (0)1722 716 376 Fax: +44 (0)1722 716 881
e-mail: sales@francisfrith.co.uk **www.francisfrith.com**